Summary & Analysis

Fire and Fury

Inside the Trump White House

Dr. Michael Wolff

Summarized by Black Book

Copyright © 2018 by Nirvan Publishing, All rights reserved

All rights reserved. No part of this publication may be reproduced, distributed, or transmitted in any form or by any means, including photocopying, recording, or other electronic or mechanical methods, without the prior written permission of the publisher, except in the case of brief quotations embodied in critical reviews and certain other noncommercial uses permitted by copyright law. For permission, direct requests to the publisher, addressed "Attention: Permissions Coordinator," at the address below.

Distribution of this book without the prior permission of the author is illegal, and therefore punishable by law.

Disclaimer

Legal Notice: - The author and publisher of this book and the accompanying materials have used their best efforts in preparing the material. The author and publisher make no representation or warranties with respect to the accuracy, applicability, fitness or completeness of the contents of this book. The information contained in this book is strictly for educational purposes. Therefore, if you wish to apply ideas contained in this book, you are taking full responsibility for your actions.

The author and publisher disclaim any warranties (express or implied), merchantability, or fitness for any particular purpose. The author and publisher shall in no event be held liable to any party for any direct, indirect, punitive, special, incidental or other consequential damages arising directly or indirectly from any use of this material, which is provided "as is", and without warranties.

As always, the advice of a competent legal, tax, accounting or other professional should be sought. The author and publisher do not warrant the performance, effectiveness or applicability of any sites listed or linked to in this book. All links are for information purposes only and are not warranted for content, accuracy or any other implied or explicit purpose.

Table of Contents

Summary of Fire and Fury: Inside the Trump White House 9

Prologue: Ailes and Bannon 13

Chapter One: Election Day 14

Chapter Two: Trump Tower 16

Chapter Three: Day One 18

Chapter Four: Bannon 20

Chapter Five: Jarvanka 22

Chapter Six: At Home 24

Chapter Seven: Russia 25

Chapter Eight: Org Chart 27

Chapter Nine: CPAC 29

Chapter Ten: Goldman 31

Chapter Eleven: Wiretap 33

Chapter Twelve: Repeal and Replace 34

Chapter Thirteen: Bannon Agonistes 36

Chapter Fourteen: Situation Room 38

Chapter Fifteen: Media 40

Chapter Sixteen: Comey 42

Chapter Seventeen: Abroad and at Home 44

Chapter Eighteen: Bannon Redux 46

Chapter Nineteen: Mika Who? 48

Chapter Twenty: McMaster and Scaramucci 50

Chapter Twenty-One: Bannon and Scaramucci 52

Chapter Twenty-Two: General Kelly 53

Epilogue: Bannon and Trump 55
Discussion Questions 56
Author Information 58
More Books by Michael Wolff 59

Summary of Fire and Fury: Inside the Trump White House

This book is a non-fiction book written from the perspective of Michael Wolff. It covers the events and people surrounding Donald Trump from May 2016 through the first 200 days or so of his Presidency. It is based on conversations Wolff had with the President and the people surrounding him.

Through the eyes of Trump's closest aides and family members, the book begins with the understanding they all share: Trump will lose the election and everyone will get what they want. However, once Trump is president, everything changes. Trump's White House quickly becomes a power struggle, mostly between Bannon, Trump's campaign manager, and Kushner, Trump's son-in-law. The question is not who will control Trump, because he is uncontrollable, but rather who can get the last word in. Thus, in some ways, this book is more about Bannon and Kushner than about Trump.

As expected, having a White House with two competing parties without a leader to make final decisions resulted in a President who appeared bipolar. Kushner started out by hiring a team of other Jews to help him. In retaliation, Bannon started to arrange for leaks about Kushner and Ivanka, and they returned the favor. In time, it was clear that Bannon was losing the war. To placate everyone, Trump agreed not to fire Bannon. However, Trump also promoted Kushner and Ivanka at the same time.

By the first 100 days into the Presidency, there were three separate PR teams in the White House. One for Trump, one for Bannon and one for Kushner and Ivanka. Thus, when Trump fired Comey and Muller took over as the head of the Russia investigation, the White House could not get itself organized to mount a solid defense. Eventually, the war came to a head. Trump overheard Bannon screaming at Hope Hicks, one of the people who was helping Kushner and Ivanka manage Trump. Trump himself was completely confused.

The situation was reversing. It was Kushner and Ivanka who had pushed for Comey to be fired, and that was turning into a hot mess. Their solution - hire Scaramucci as the Director of Communications - also backfired. Bannon was doing well. At least, he was doing well until Trump hired Kelly to be his new Chief of Staff. Determined to settle the quarrel that was tearing the White House apart, Bannon had to go.

Chapter-By-Chapter Summary

Prologue: Ailes and Bannon

A 66-year-old Roger Ailes waited for Steve Bannon to make it to dinner. Ailes, the former head of Fox News and long-time friend of Donald Trump, considered himself an expert on politics. Yet when Trump offered him the position to head his campaign, Ailes refused, leaving the opening to Bannon. Now that Trump was president, Ailes was hoping to use their friendship to help him regain a position of influence.

Three hours late, the 63-year-old Bannon finally arrived for dinner. Wolff describes him as "curiously able to embrace Trump, while at the same time suggesting he did not take him entirely seriously". The conversation that ensued between Ailes and Bannon over dinner suggested that both parties thought Trump didn't really understand politics, and maybe wasn't smart enough to try.

Chapter One: Election Day

Kellyanne Conway was Trump's campaign manager. She was also completely prepared for Trump to lose the 2016 Presidential election and thought she'd laid out the pieces correctly to land herself a job on cable TV. There was no need to worry about whether Trump was prepared to be president, because he wasn't going to be.

Trump himself was skeptical about the campaign, calling everyone in it a "loser" and refusing to invest his own money. Eventually, his son in law, Jared Kushner, convinced Trump to give his own campaign a $10 million loan.

Melania Trump thought Trump could win. However, she was also terrified by the prospect. She was rich and pampered, and she never had to deal with the other members of Trump's family or the press. Trump promised that he wouldn't become President.

In fact, everyone in Trump's inner circle was betting on the fact that Trump wouldn't win. To them, winning was losing out on the plans they'd already carefully crafted for themselves. When Election Day finally rolled around, and Trump was elected president, it was unhappy chaos.

Chapter Two: Trump Tower

People who had spent their entire lives dismissive of Trump were now finding that they had to reevaluate their relationship with Trump. Since he had managed the unimaginable miracle of becoming President, could he possibly also handle the responsibilities of the job? Despite his ignorance on almost every subject, he somehow had the right words to make people instinctively trust him.

Unfortunately, the problems were more than lack of knowledge. Among his associates, Trump was known for calling up wives and trying to convince them to sleep with him. Even beyond his lack of moral scruples, he seemed to lack all ability to link cause and effect.

This trouble with planning extended into transitioning from the Obama government to the Trump administration. Trump set up shop in Trump Tower, and refused to go to Washington. Everyone would have to come to him. Alarmingly, he also offered people jobs in his Administration within minutes of meeting them, ignorant of their qualifications or even their character.

Finding a Chief of Staff was tricky. His top choice, longtime friend Tom Barrack, told Trump there was no way he could sort out his businesses and find capable hands for all of them in time. Trump's next choice, his son-in-law Kushner, seemed willing enough. However, the rest of his advisors told Trump that he could not simply hire his family. Third in line was Chris Christie, who seemed eager for the role. This time, Trump's daughter Ivanka stepped in. As Christie was the one who had sent her father-in-law to jail, it would bring serious discord to the family if Christie was named the President's Chief of Staff.

After his first three choices were nixed, Trump favored Bannon. After all, this was the aide who had won him the election. Washington wanted Reince Priebus. Vaguely political but definitely Republican, Priebus was eventually given the job. Yet Barrack, Kushner and Bannon could all still access Trump at their leisure: Priebus was Chief of Staff in name only.

Then the Steele dossier broke, suggesting Trump had colluded with Russia to win the election. What was supposed to be a routine press conference - the first since Trump was elected - became a joke.

Chapter Three: Day One

If you wanted to give Trump advice, but didn't want to talk to Trump, Kushner was the man to see. By the time Trump took office, Kushner was convinced that Trump needed to make amends with the intelligence community.

Trump himself found his inauguration disappointing because no A-list star would participate. Throughout the event it was obvious he was fighting with his wife, and the day which was supposed to filled with love as he was welcomed as President was instead filled with disappointment. The aggrieved speech Bannon had written for the inaugural address seemed to fit Trump's mood perfectly.

Bannon had decided that Trump's relationship with the media was doomed. Trump was unable to stick to his script and get the facts right, and thus the media was always going to crucify Trump. The speech marked the first instance of what was going to be an ongoing theme: Trump governed through fits of anger.

But Kushner had convinced Trump that the CIA should be a priority, and so to the CIA Trump went to deliver a reconciliatory speech about how good their new director was. Instead, he rambled like a demented parrot about many different topics, confusing everyone who was listening.

Chapter Four: Bannon

Bannon claimed his office in the White House before the Inaugural march was even finished. He set about removing all the furniture, save a desk and a chair for himself. There would be no meetings held in his office.

An odd creature, Bannon had lived an undistinguished life. He went to college at Virginia Tech, then joined the Navy, before doing a stint at the Pentagon before leaving the Navy. Harvard Business school followed, then a job at Goldman Sachs in which he never got very far. He became an entrepreneur, but never made it big, eventually getting hired by a bunch of failing companies where he only seemed to make their downfall occur faster.

Finally, he drifted into conservative media, possibly because the barriers to entry were much lower than liberal media. There, he met the Mercers. The father and daughter pair were as rich as they were odd, and thus fully willing to fund anything that agreed with their unusual ideals. Thus, when Trump came into the picture, it didn't much matter to Bannon what his ideals were. Trump was rich, and Bannon was there to facilitate what he wanted.

An entrepreneur still, Bannon knew he needed to strike while the iron was hot. Previously, he had developed a list of 200 executive orders to be enacted during the first 100 days of Trump's presidency. The most important one pertained to illegal immigration, and thus it was already drafted.

Under the chaos of Trump's alternate beliefs regarding his inauguration and the oddity of the speech to the CIA, Bannon was able to get an executive order banning most Muslims from entering the US signed. No one was notified, including the organizations responsible for enacting the order.

Why? Because Bannon believed that the best way to beat the liberals who opposed Trump was to drive them crazy.

Chapter Five: Jarvanka

No-one thought it was a good idea for Kushner to take a job at the White House. As Trump's son-in-law, he would have plenty of access. However, as both Kushner and Ivanka knew, proximity to Trump was everything. While he never really listened to anyone, the fact someone was present did seem to influence him.

Kushner and Trump were both more alike than they realized. Raised in privilege, they sought more prestige, and both decided the way to gain it was via the media. While Trump did this via media infamy and then The Apprentice, Kushner simply bought a newspaper. After driving the New York Observer into the ground, he achieved almost as much media infamy as his father-in-law.

Yet even though Trump and Kushner were similar in attitude, Kushner could not guide Trump, as evidenced by the fiasco with the Mexican president less than a week after Trump's inaugural address. Kushner had a meeting all arranged, but he could not stop Trump from one last inflammatory tweet. The Mexican president cancelled.

Ivanka's relationship with her father was devoid of the anger many of her peers felt towards their fathers. She knew she was her own product, and her product was now to be the first daughter. Royalty.

So, she did what other would not. She met with people who were used to Washington and the politics which enveloped it. Ivanka was not going to be just a novelty, she was going to stand with her husband to shift the stance of the White House away from the antagonism it seemed bent on.

Chapter Six: At Home

Despite the mice and the cockroaches, for most people the White House is palatial. Not so for Trump. Used to being surrounded by servants who knew his every routine, moving to the White House was a trial for Trump.

On the other hand, Trump loved meeting with the business councils that were assembled to meet with him. The fancy handouts and the precisely choreographed schedules suited him perfectly. This was his world, where he was talking to people he respected and who were giving him their respect in return.

However, while the media in the past had always portrayed Presidents with a sense of togetherness they may not have deserved, they refused to accord Trump with the same sense of respect. Trump was outraged and desperately wanted to find the leak that explained where the media was getting his information from. He never considered it might be late-night phone calls he made complaining about everyone and everything to anyone he happened to be able to get in contact with.

Chapter Seven: Russia

First conceived of about six months before Trump was ever sworn in, the Russia conspiracy had many different possible theories as to how it came about.

1. Trump is drawn to male authority, like Putin. Knowing this, why wouldn't the Russians try to get him elected?

2. Trump is involved in a cabal of dirty money laundering, which is how the Russians got connected with him. Indeed, he has had business dealings with several Russians with various degrees of tarnished reputation.

3. Trump and Putin got together to hack the Democratic National Committee.

4. The Russians have something on Trump and are thus blackmailing him.

5. Trump wanted respect, and that was why he took the beauty pageant to Russia, even though it got him nowhere.

Inside the White House, even six months after Trump became President, the worry was not about whether Trump had colluded with the Russians. Thee worry was that any investigation would stumble upon something Trump or Kushner were guilty of.

Twenty-four days into the Presidency, when Flynn, the National Security Advisor, was caught in a lie about talking to the Russians, Trump was adamant that he not be fired. However, the rest of his advisors disagreed, and eventually came up with a reason Trump could accept. The first senior White House staffer was gone, less than a month into the Presidency.

Chapter Eight: Org Chart

Trump wanted everyone in every meeting. The Oval office wasn't a place for him to get work done. It was the place everyone tried to do their work. In fact, from Trump's perspective, if something did not happen under his nose, it had not happened at all.

At the center of this chaos was not Priebus, despite his completely honorary title of Chief of Staff. Neither was it Bannon or Kushner, the two men vying to be the power behind the throne. No. It was the deputy chief of staff, Katie Walsh. Her entire career had been in Washington. She knew who had the power and how the game was played.

One of her first observations was that in the Trump White House, rather than Trump giving orders and people doing their best to make it happen, top aides made suggestions to Trump and tried to get him to believe he was the one who had come up with the idea.

Because of this, much of the policy formulated by the Trump White House was done based on the written and oral record of the many speeches Trump made while campaigning. There was no other choice. It was impossible to get the President to concentrate on any one matter for any length of time.

Bannon pushed for isolationism, Priebus supported classic Republican values, and Kushner counselled moderation. In the middle, Walsh watched as the President bounced between these three like a ball. By the end of the second week of the Presidency, all three men were in deep conflict with each other.

Thus, by the end of the first month, each man had developed their own weapons. For both Bannon and Kushner, it was the media. While neither gave on the record interviews, both arranged for leaks to happen. It was a witch hunt where everyone was both hunter and witch.

In early March, Walsh confronted Kushner, and asked him to give her three things Trump wanted to focus on. Kushner agreed; that was probably something the Trump Presidency should decide on.

Chapter Nine: CPAC

The Conservative Political Action Conference had considered itself the true core of the conservative movement for decades, and as such had never really taken Trump seriously. But now Trump was President, which meant he had to be embraced. Worse, Richard Spencer and his alt-right white supremacism were coming along on Trump's coattails.

Bannon and Priebus were part of a panel together on the first day, an opportunity for Bannon to make subtle and sometimes not-so-subtle jabs at Kushner while also suggesting that he was allying with Priebus. Bannon was suave, with carefully crafted answers to questions, while Priebus bumbled around.

Trump's speech the subsequent day was piles of free-association and ramblings. His staffers were always careful to keep their expressions neutral, waiting to see how the audience reacted before allowing themselves any reaction of their own.

Spencer, now banned from the conference, was nonetheless talking to the press any chance he got. Claiming Bannon and Trump to be open to the idea of racism and the people that espoused it, Spencer was never lacking for an audience. According to him, the Trump movement was always a white supremacist movement, and one that could never have existed without the alt-right to lead the way.

Chapter Ten: Goldman

Increasingly, Kushner felt as though Bannon was trying to get under his skin, particularly by using the fact that he was a Jew against him. Trump, at least partially, was part of this too - by giving Kushner the task of overseeing the affairs in the Middle-East, he was putting his son-in-law to the test.

So, the orthodox Jew struck back by bringing in another Jew: Gary Cohn, the former president of Goldman Sachs. Cohn became Trump's economic advisor, and he was the opposite of Bannon. Bannon pushed his ideas and his agenda, while Cohn read the room and acted accordingly. The question was, would Bannon's headlong rush destroy him before he could destroy the alliance Kushner and Cohn had built?

Ivanka, in her own way, was also involved. She convinced another Jew and employee of Goldman Sachs to join the White House: Gina Powell. Ivanka convinced Powell that the four of them could really shape the White House and redirect it towards reason and moderation.

The test came during Trump's second month in office. He was going to speak to Congress. Not only was the text of the speech going to be released beforehand, but there would be a teleprompter and there was no crowd to give Trump the feedback he craved. For once, it worked. Even the media agreed that Trump had managed to be Presidential.

Chapter Eleven: Wiretap

Unfortunately for the team Kushner and Ivanka had assembled to try and manage Trump, their victory was to be short-lived. Three people in the Trump administration had now been linked to Kislyak, a Russian diplomat. Potentially with some judicious leaks from Bannon, this included Kushner.

Trump didn't see it that way at all. From his perspective, everything about Russia was coming from vengeful holdovers from the Obama administration. Thus, the tweets poured out, accusing Obama of illegal activity without any factual evidence to back it up.

Chapter Twelve: Repeal and Replace

Trump was oddly apathetic about Obamacare. In fact, he was overheard to say, "Why can't Medicare just cover everyone?" Bannon, wisely, took a back seat to this discussion and let Paul Ryan, the Speaker of the House, talk to Trump about it.

Thus, it was Ryan who came up with the idea of repealing the Affordable Care Act while replacing it with something else. Trump happily told him he could run with it.

This drew Bannon up short. If Trump was willing to fob off major policy choices, then Bannon would need to assemble a team who could draft legislation in line with his idea of what Trump's policies should look like. Kushner took the opposite road. Trump could not decide between policy approaches and thus perhaps it was better to just let difficult policy choices make themselves.

However, Ryan was just as uninterested in writing a healthcare reform bill as Trump. So, while all the while assuring the president that it was a done deal, Ryan quietly outsourced the writing to lobbyists and insurance companies.

By mid-March, it was clear the healthcare bill was not doing well. Cohn joined the efforts, seemingly against his wishes. Bannon in turn was merciless, calling reporters and blaming everyone except himself. Despite Ryan calling the White House to tell Trump he was short the votes he needed for the bill to pass, Bannon pushed for the vote to happen, wanting the failure to occur so he could use it as ammunition against others. Trump hesitated, and Ryan was able to cancel the vote.

Walsh, completely frustrated, was out the door by the end of the week. Another senior staffer was gone.

Chapter Thirteen: Bannon Agonistes

Bannon had a dream. He was going to restore the privileges of the working class by making America more isolationist. The rest of the White House allowed the idea, but disparaged it.

It didn't help Bannon's case that he often referred to himself as "President Bannon" and took every opportunity he got to bomb press photos and disparage Ivanka. Despite his blustering, he was in a bad way. Trump began to harshly disparage him to everyone, and eventually it was obvious: Bannon was an alt-right supporter, yet he was answering to Kushner and Ivanka, who were both entitled Democrats. It was the epitome of irony.

The Mercers, determined to protect their investment, met with Trump. However, Trump didn't like either of them. Seeking advice elsewhere, he was told that firing Bannon was inevitable and that it was impossible, depending on who he talked to.

In the background, Kushner was doing everything he could to get rid of Bannon. Without him, Kushner and the rest of the Jews in the White House might be able to turn the Trump Presidency around and into something respectable.

In the end, Trump agreed not to fire Bannon immediately. In return, Kushner was promoted and given more power and Ivanka was given an official role in the White House. Yet, because Bannon remained, so did his belief that he was destined to be in the White House and his goals would yet be accomplished.

Chapter Fourteen: Situation Room

No one was sure how Trump would react when the news reached the White House of a chemical weapons attack in Syria. Trump was random and unsettlingly capricious, especially when it came to foreign policy.

The trouble Ivanka and Powell were having was that Trump got plenty of information. Unfortunately, all of it was informal through the news channels on TV and various individuals who told him want he wanted to hear. There was no way to get Trump to listen to details or expert analysis of problems.

Despite this, a presentation was assembled and given to Trump. Unfortunately, it didn't appear that he was getting the seriousness of what was going on. What he did appear to be doing, for the first time in a while, was listening to Bannon. While everyone else was urging Trump to act and thus show strength, Bannon pointed out that nothing good had ever come from the US interfering in the Middle East. His advice? Let them fix their own mess.

Yet Ivanka and Powell managed to break through, by showing Trump pictures of the children who had died in the attack. By the end of the day, Trump was all for a military solution. It had taken all day, but they had finally managed to get Trump to make the decision they wanted all along.

Chapter Fifteen: Media

Trump listened to the news constantly on TV, often on replaying segments. At Bannon's urging, he was always making statements designed make the conservative media happy and inflame the liberal media. This was what Trump could not get: anything that made one happy would invariably make the other upset. To Trump, the media should love anyone who was famous and wealthy. He was certainly wealthy and, as the President, he couldn't possibly get any more famous. Thus, he was constantly upset because from his perspective, the media should all like him.

Rather than making the White House cohesive, this had the opposite effect. Trump had a personal PR person in the form of Hope Hicks, whose sole task seemed to be having long meetings with Trump. The goal was for Trump to get some positive press on the front page of the New York Times. Kushner and Ivanka hired their own PR person in turn, as did Bannon.

Overshadowing all of this was the White House correspondents' dinner, set for the night that marked Trump's first 100 days as President. Trump was initially insistent that he could do it. After all, he'd appeared on SNL in 2015, and that had been great, hadn't it? Bannon eventually convinced Trump not to attend, and everyone breathed a sigh of relief.

Chapter Sixteen: Comey

Kushner and Ivanka were terrified that Comey, the Director of the FBI, was going to find something about Trump, or the extended Trump businesses, that was going to get them all in trouble. It didn't help that the other billionaires Trump and the duo talked to were all convinced that the Department of Justice was set against them.

Initially, Bannon and Don McGahn, the White House counsel, thought they had talked the President out of firing Comey. Unfortunately, when a weekend getaway was ruined by rain, Trump was stuck inside with Kushner and Ivanka. They convinced him to change his mind. A few days later, Trump acted on his own initiative and fired Comey.

However, in doing so, he made an enemy of Rod Rosenstein, the Deputy Attorney General. Since the Attorney General had already recused himself from any investigation due a possible conflict, it fell to Rosenstein to decide whether the same was true for him. Rosenstein decided that he couldn't be unbiased, and thus he appointed the prior Director of the FBI, Robert Mueller, to lead the Russia investigation.

Chapter Seventeen: Abroad and at Home

Despite the ongoing problems with Comey and Muller, Trump believed he was one win away from everything going his way. The healthcare reform had completely fallen through, and Trump was uninterested in smaller pieces of legislation.

It was Kushner who finally brought him the big solution: the Crown Prince of Saudi Arabia, Mohammed bin Salman bin Abdulaziz Al Saud, was willing to play ball and try to create peace in the Middle East. In turn, Trump would visit Saudi Arabia for his first visit overseas.

Yet, even though the Saudis seemed willing to work with Trump, the press was not: the headlines still spoke of Comey and Muller. Bannon decided to create a separate legal and communications team to deal with any press on the Russia issue. Ideally, the White House would never issue another statement about it.

Unfortunately for Bannon, top law firms wanted nothing to do with it. The younger staff didn't like

Trump, the older partners were worried that Trump wouldn't pay, and everyone worried that Trump would get unreasonably angry with them and publicly humiliate the firm.

Chapter Eighteen: Bannon Redux

With Kushner and Ivanka failing twice in a row, team Bannon was once again ascending. He got Trump to withdraw from the Paris climate agreement, and he began telling the President that it was imperative that Trump distance himself from Kushner and Ivanka. Everyone was trying to cover their own backs, and was thus clamming up, not wanting to get drawn in.

Trump, told that he could not take his ire out on Muller, instead focused it on Sessions, the Attorney General who was never supposed to have recused himself in the first place. Bannon strongly disagree with the President on this, and thus found himself in the firing line as well.

Everyone was blaming everyone else. Kushner and Ivanka lacked the necessary experience to advise the President, Bannon was too harsh in his policies and had made too many enemies, and Priebus should have been doing a better job at insulating the President from himself.

When Comey testified before the Senate, he was precise, honorable and detailed. In other words, everything Trump wasn't. When Sessions testified a few days later, he appeared nervous and out of his depth. Bannon knew it wasn't going well. Kushner did not.

Chapter Nineteen: Mika Who?

Mika Brzezinski was the co-host of a breakfast show Trump regularly watched. At the beginning of his Presidency, Mika and her co-host had been upbeat and generally in favor of what was going on. However, the tone of the show had been distinctly less positive of late. Trump, in return, had stopped watching it, irate that people he had helped make media stars were making a living out of giving him negative press. Yet, every morning he asked Hope Hicks what latest episode had said.

This White House was odd. Unlike prior Presidencies which could barely hold the public's attention, Trump's very nature seemed to hold everyone captive. What crazy thing is he going to do next? It was oddly addicting, with each new fiasco seeming to cancel out the next.

Of course, this is when the news got ahold of the information that, during the Trump campaign, Don Trump Jr., Kushner, and Paul Manafort had met with a group of Russia with dubious credentials. No one believed this meeting could have taken place without Trump being aware of what was going on.

In a change of events, being excluded from Trump's communication meetings was now an exalted status. It meant you were likely clear of any mud that was about to fall. Trump insisted to everyone he could that the meeting at Trump Tower was not about Hillary Clinton, ignoring any evidence to the contrary.

Much to the lawyer's dismay, Trump remained convinced that it was acceptable to lie to the media, which he did. Thus, the trick Bannon had tried to play by creating a legal wall around the President had broken.

Bannon, furious, was determined that the investigation would find Kushner or, even better, both Kushner and Ivanka at fault. As Trump continued to rail at Sessions, Bannon got more and more angry, eventually declaring all-out war against Kushner and Ivanka in front of a highly confused Trump.

Chapter Twenty: McMaster and Scaramucci

An issue which had plagued Trump from day one was Afghanistan. Bannon, in typical Bannon fashion, wanted to cause as much trouble as possible while doing as little as possible. McMaster, the three-star general in charge of the national security council, told the President that they would need to send 50,000-60,000 more troops if they wanted to win the war.

In the end, it was Powell and Ivanka who came up with a solution. Sent a few thousand, no more than seven thousand, to hold the line. Realizing that the President would never go for the larger surge, McMaster agreed to reduce his numbers. However, in a meeting presenting this to him, Trump lost it. Bannon was certain he had finally triumphed over Kushner and Ivanka.

However, the couple had a play in the works. They were certain part of their problem was that the White House communications staff was not being aggressive enough in their defense. The solution would be to appoint someone as a communications director who understood where they were coming from and would go to bat for them.

After much searching, both on their part and Trump's, they settled on Anthony Scaramucci. He'd been seeking a top job in the White House since Trump won the election. Oddly enough, he managed to convince the first family of his loyalty even though he'd rooted for Obama and Hillary Clinton prior to that. Bannon thought it was simply more evidence that Kushner and Ivanka were losing.

Chapter Twenty-One: Bannon and Scaramucci

The President told the head of his communication's team that Scaramucci was becoming the Director of Communications, the man, with evident relief, resigned. Oddly enough, Scaramucci's appointment also made him Priebus' boss. Thus, when Scaramucci started to blame Priebus for leaking information about him, Priebus suggested that Trump begin looking for a replacement Chief of Staff.

Scaramucci then proceeded to call a reporter from the New Yorker and complain about his life. The resulting article was a disgrace, and Priebus wondered if he had resigned too early. He talked to the President about when he should leave, and the President told him to take his time. A few minutes after the meeting ended, Priebus' phone pinged him: Trump had just tweeted that he had fired Priebus and was making John Kelly his new Chief of Staff.

This tweet was also the first time Kelly had heard of his appointment. Six days later when he was sworn in, Kelly fired Scaramucci.

Chapter Twenty-Two: General Kelly

Trump and his entourage left for Bedminster. While the President had instructed that time should be set aside for golf, he was also equally insistent that this was a working trip. As such, Kelly had decided there were two issues the President needed to work on: Bannon's team and Kushner and Ivanka's team. At least one of them had to go, and ideally both.

Kelly's first move was to make Kushner and Ivanka understand that they needed to go through him to talk to Trump. They could not keep jumping the line. Bannon, still not invited to go to Bedminster, sent Kelly his resignation, trying to force Kelly into taking stronger action against Kushner and Ivanka.

While this was unfolding around Trump, the neo-Nazi protest was taking place in Charlottesville. Trump's staff hurriedly composed a tweet about unity and let the matter lie until Trump's infamous words on "hatred, bigotry and violence on many sides". While his staff again hurried to make clear that included white supremacists, Trump himself refused to actually say the words. It wasn't until several days later that Ivanka convinced her father to make a televised statement condemning racism.

However, it was less than a day later when Trump recanted, saying there was blame on both sides for the violence. The rest of the world was aghast, and to save themselves, everyone in the public sector who was tied to Trump had to disavow his actions.

During this, Bannon made a call to a reporter to talk about the threat China posed. During the call, Bannon couldn't help but be himself: Trump was weak, but that was okay, because Bannon was going to be there to push Trump in the right direction. Still furious about the book, The Devil's Bargain, which credited Bannon for Trump becoming President, Bannon was fired as soon as Trump read the article based on the conversation Bannon had with the reporter.

Epilogue: Bannon and Trump

Bannon was out of the White House, but he wasn't out of politics. For better or worse, he now considered himself the leader of the alt-right political movement. Trump had simply been a figurehead, and Bannon could just as easily take over.

Most of the senior staff had by now realized that Trump wasn't magic, he was simply an idiot who had gotten lucky. Anyone who was more mature and stable than Trump he disliked, or even hated. Trump had even stopped defending his family.

On the other hand, Bannon had declared that he was going to run for President in 2020. He was meeting with all the right people, and, in true Bannon style, trying to recruit people who would cause waves. From his perspective, Trump was becoming little more than a footnote in the history of the alt-right.

Discussion Questions

1. Why do you think Trump appealed to so many voters?

2. Do you think Kushner and Ivanka were correct to take jobs in the White House?

3. What effect do you think Kushner and Ivanka have had on the Trump White House? Do you think it was mostly positive or negative?

4. What effect do you think Bannon had on the Trump White House? Do you think it was mostly positive or negative?

5. One of themes throughout the book is Trump's need to be admired. Why do you think he is that way?

6. In the book, Trump is described as "post-literate" because he hates to read and much prefers to get his information in auditory format. Yet, one of his favorite forms of communication is tweeting, and he often writes long tweets. Discuss.

7. Why do you think so many senior officials left the Trump White House? Do you think that was a good thing, or a bad one?

8. Based on how this book illustrates the Trump White House, do you think Trump could elected again in 2020?

9. Many people in the book, besides Trump, aired the possibility of running for President themselves, most notably Bannon and Ivanka. Do you think either of them would make a good President? Why or why not?

10. Based on the analysis in the book, which of Trump's decisions do you disagree with the most? Why?

11. Based on the analysis in the book, which of Trump's decisions do you agree with the most? Why?

12. Throughout the book, Trump is shown to be suggest able and random. Do you think he was always this way? Or, as the book suggests towards the end, are his ramblings getting worse because he has a progressive form of dementia?

Author Information

Michael Wolff is a journalist who regularly writes columns for USA Today and The Hollywood Reporter. He was born in New Jersey and went to school at Columbia University. While still studying, he worked as a copy boy for The New York Times.

His writing has had a mixed reception over the years. While some find Wolff's critiques to be on point and valid, others have accused him of focusing on power players without regard for facts or firsthand knowledge of the events.

Wolff has twice won the National Magazine Award and has received a Mirror Award for Best Commentary: Traditional Media.

More Books by Michael Wolff

Television Is the New Television: The Unexpected Triumph of Old Media in the Digital Age is a non-fiction book about how experts predicted the fall of old-school media, such as newspapers, and how in turn they have been wrong. As new media, such as Netflix, fails to overtake the giants of old, such as the New York Times, how will that influence the future of the internet? You can read it for yourself here.

Burn Rate: How I Survived the Gold Rush Years on the Internet is an autobiographical book about Michael Wolff's time as a digital entrepreneur. As the title suggests, he focuses on the burn rate of his company: how much his company was losing every month. You can read it for yourself here.

The Man Who Owns the News: Inside the Secret World of Rupert Murdoch is a non-fiction book about Rupert Murdoch, the man who owns The New York Post and the Wall Street Journal. Written by Michael Wolff after thousands of hours interviewing Murdoch's family and close associates, the book paints an intimate portrait of both Murdoch and the dynasty he has established. You can read it for yourself here.

For more books by Michael Wolff, look here.

Made in the USA
Columbia, SC
13 July 2025